INTRODUCTION TO
ROY NOBLE'S BOOK OF NICKNAMES

I was once told that in Iceland people were listed in the telephone directory according to occupation. This was because of the difficulty in passing on surnames from one generation to the other, for example, Morgan Johanson's son Ingemar would become Ingemar Morganson.

Wales could have a similar complication if ever the use of 'ap', meaning 'son of', again becomes fashionable when naming new male babies. The telephone directory listing would make interesting reading.

Rhys ap Dafydd's son Idwal would become Idwal ap Rhys and Idwal's son Meredith would be listed as Meredith ap Idwal....I think.

The listing would probably use the first name as a basis for alphabetical order and Rhys, Idwal and Meredith would be nowhere near each other in any directory. The staff at the records office for births, marriages and deaths would also be under stress whenever an enquiry came in.

There is, however, another possibility to add colour and glorious confusion to Welsh name listings.

The various tribes of Jones, Evans, Thomas, Williams, Jenkins, Cadwaladar etc. etc. could be listed according to their local stamp of recognition...their nicknames.

Roy the Chat

These nicknames have been part of Welsh social classification, division and folklore for decades, and many have been listed on previous occasions.

They merit re-appraisal however, because they're still there. Whether the nicknames come from a job, a family, a trait, a particular prowess, or a personal habit, they're still recognised and appreciated.

Amongst those included in this book are ones that are old and well known, but which are still relevant. There are also new ones, current ones, innovative ones and resurrected ones.

The list was completed from contributions sent in by listeners to The Roy Noble Show on BBC Radio Wales. To them all, I give my thanks. I did think of listing all contributors as well, but if I had left any out there would have been trouble, and anyway, some were sent in anonymously.

My thanks indeed to Gren for bringing all these names to life, as only he can with his special talent. Enjoy them, and if you can think of any more such names please use the fly sheet at the back of this book and send them in, and then we can think of filling up Volume 2.

£4.99

Published By

Western Mail Books
Thomson House, Havelock Street, Cardiff CF1 1XR
Telephone Cardiff 01222 583583/223333
Registered Number 46946 England

Edited by John Cosslett

Designed and Typeset by Andrew Jones, Carol Williams

Printed by Mid Wales Litho Ltd, New Inn, Pontypool, Gwent

British Library Cataloguing-in-Publication Data.

A catalogue of this book is available from The National Library
of Wales and The British Library

ISBN1-900477-04-1

Tom Evans Hard

A corruption of Evans y wlad -
Evans from the country.

Gladly

A polar bear in Whipsnade Zoo with a turn in its eye - a lovely-natured animal and a great favourite with the children. From the hymn - "Gladly the cross I'd bear."

Nap

He looked like Napoleon.

Jelly

His initials were J.L. and he
was very fat.

Dickie Peg

Had one leg.

Exocet

*You could see him coming but it was
too late to avoid him.*

Wenvoe

A very tall, extremely thin man who lived not too far from the TV mast in the area.

Sack-em-Jack

No second chance with this manager of Abercynon Colliery.

R-Plus

His name was Rhys Reginald Rhys..

Luigi Vanilla

Always recommended the vanilla
ice-cream as being particularly
good that day.

Metal Moth

A welding foreman who would pick holes in everything.

George Blood

Always carried a first-aid box in
K. District of Albion Colliery.

Lame Duck

Had a bad arm.

Pugh the Pru

Insurance agent - Treforest - but he actually
collected for the Co-op.

Ivor Apples & Pears

Real name Ivor Orchard, from Pontypridd.

Dai Russia

Local Communist

Dai Full Pelt

Always running – and saying
"Can't stop, got to go".

Egg on Legs

Very short and round.

Billy Shake-um

Clock and watch repairer.
He would shake the watch and say
"Come back in a fortnight."

Juanita Chiquita

She became a cheek-eater after her only remaining
tooth was extracted.

Will Ten to Two

Walked with feet at an angle.

Duckie

Donald Thomas.

Johnny Header

Tested a safety harness by jumping off
the jib of a crane. He dropped to the floor
but was unhurt

Wing-nut Williams

Had protruding ears.

Billy Cash Down

Purchased everything with cash - had nothing on tick.

Em Fat

Always used the word "emphatically."

Seagull

Ate a great deal.

Joe Filter

Had a thin moustache.

Shoni Gladys

John Evans whose wife was Gladys.

John the Box

Undertaker John Lewis.

Dai Door

Doorman at Glyncoch Social Club.

Dai Ginger

Red hair.

Tom Cockles

Tom Marshman who sold cockles.

Bryn Chops

His wife said he was the only man who could talk under water - from Treforest.

The Duke

real name Will Wellington

Dai Pretty Trousers

A barber who wore a different pair of trousers each day under his short white coat and would ask, "Do you like my pretty trousers?"

Two-eyes Lewis

Worked in Albion Colliery – and had an
eye tattoed on each buttock.

Bob Tink

Had relatives who were tinkers.

Les Doll's Hair

Had bright, curly blond hair - from Matthewstown, Mountain Ash.

John Dwywaith

Welsh for twice (John Johns).

Conger

Slippery as an eel.

Keith Curl

Had a quiff.

Clogger

Wore heavy boots.

Will 18 months

Will Lloyd - whose ear was half severed in
a pit accident.

Dai Grass

The groundsman.

Spike

6' 3" and weighed only 8st

Tommy Bandit

Always on the machines at Llantwit
Fardre Rugby Club.

Dai Quiet
Wedding

Wore a slipper to his wedding
following a foot injury.

Dai Vindaloo

Real name - David Currie.

Bong

Had a habit of tapping people
on the head and saying "Bong!"

Arkie

Real name Gabriel (archangel).

Sharky Davies

A bookmaker in Merthyr.

Herbie Good Boy

An overman at Coegnant Colliery who used the term "good boy" with every instruction.

Annie Walk Nicely

As her mother was always
telling her as a child.

Milk Bottle

A gentleman in Cymmer who is always
standing on the doorstep.

Danny Bang-bang

A shot-firer at Maerdy Colliery - he would
shout "Bang-bang" when he was ready to fire.

Lambeth Walk

A policeman in Pontycymer in the late 1940s who had a strange gait - leaning backwards and throwing his legs forward.

'ELLO 'ELLO 'ELLO!

Jim Poison Pellets

An engine driver at St John's, Maesteg who would give local gardeners the pellets he used to control weeds on the railway lines.

Eddie Click

Photographer (Kenfig Hill).

Cherry

Had a red complexion.

Stan the Can

Recycles cans (Swansea).

Dai Moonshine

Eyes used to become glassy after drinking -
real name Dai Rees of Pontycymer.

Will Pebbledash

Very bad skin.

Dai One-eye

He lived in No1 'Igh Street.

Fanny
Spare-parts

A teacher whose clothes were
never co-ordinated.

Dai Cube

David Davies - a maths
master from Aberdare Boys
Grammar School.

Dai Picasso

Always used the phrase "Now let me
put you in the picture".

Tommy Gee Gee

His father was a haulage contractor,
and Tom led the horses.

Johnny Skins

Played the drums.

Jones Channel Fleet

Someone once said that he had enough children to man the Channel Fleet.

Will Both Ends

Used to be a train driver but his eyesight failed so they made him a guard.

Judy Garland

A bricklayer who worked opposite a
pub called the Rainbow. Whenever
someone needed him he was always
"Over the Rainbow".

Tommy Fire Bucket

A nightwatchman with hut and brazier.

Kipper

Owned a fresh-fish shop.

Mrs Jones London to Brighton

She used to walk up and down the road all day.

Patchy

A teacher who always wore patches on his jacket

Ap-patchy

his son

Light Socket

Had a head of hair sticking
out in a frizz.

Mary Peninsula

Always on the doorstep,
stretching out to "see!"

Mrs Noddy

A delightful old lady who agreed with everyone with a nod and a smile.

Willie Three-piece

Worked for a furniture firm.

Harpic

A Llanelli student who was "clean around the bend".

Dai Sky

Had first satellite dish in Aberystwyth.

Johnny Odd-stocking

A workshy person who used the excuse that he couldn't find his second stocking as being late for work one morning — only to find that he had put both on one leg.

Johnny Minutes

Always looking at his watch - "I'll have to go in a minute".

Ernie Black & White

He was a coal merchant but also had a milk round.

John 10 Coats

A tramp who wore several layers of clothes.

The Happy Welshman

Phil Davies, of Wine St., Pontlottyn who won a competition of not having quarrelled with his wife for one whole year. All the family also bore the nickname "Happy" for years afterwards.

Bella Blue Balls

Had beautiful blue eyes.

Ted Springs

Mr Edward Rees (a former Director of Education for Derbyshire) had a bouncy gait when walking.

Morgan the Lawyer

Mrs Elizabeth Morgan from Neath - a formidable lady who gave her opinion on everything. She owned a shop. Future generations of her family were also known by this name. No one argued with her - she knew all the answers.

Ticker

Surname was Samuels (the jeweller).

Jack Flags

Chief Superintendent John
Bunting in Colwyn Bay.

Dai Banjo

Played this instrument well.

Dai call me David

Didn't wish to be called Dai.

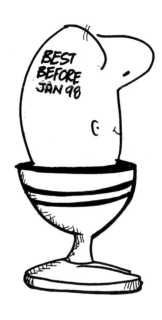

Dai Egg

Bald

became

Dai Double Yolk

when his wife had twins.

Mrs Chicken

Kept chickens under her table by wrapping
wire netting around the legs.

Hair-oil Flynn

Wore a lot of Brylcream.

Ivor the Jiver

Music teacher - Bargoed School

King Edward

Worked long hours underground.

Dai Gestive

Salesman for biscuits.

Sprout

Son of Will Cabbage.

Dai White Hunter

First to wear a white helmet
in the pit.

Dai Look-up

Pigeon fancier

Dai North

From North Wales.

Carmen Miranda

Makes a song and dance about everything.

Dai Flymo

Always hovering around.

Dai Book & Pencil

A policeman who when promoted became Dai
Book and Biro.

Dai Damp

Worked for a waterproofing company.

Dai Electric Hare

When he took his greyhounds for a walk they
always walked behind him.

Kenny Custard

Had a runny nose.

Brillo

Had wiry, curly hair.

Cu-nim

A navigator in a bomber squadron with big bushy eyebrows which resembled "cumulonimbus" clouds.

Dai Natch

Always boasted that the driving instructor told him he was a natural driver.

Dick Divine

A confirmed bachelor who loved
dancing. Real name - Richard
Griffiths. He was also very
house-proud. A paragon, in fact.

Idwal Crust

Always had a crust in his sandwich box,
became known as

Idwal Upper Crust

when he shook hands with Royalty at the
opening of the Claerwen Dam 1952.

Maggie Elastic

Lady of dubious character.

Yo-Yo

When asked how he
was - always replied
"Up and down, see."

Morris Yankee

Family had been to America.

Dai Echo

Knew everyone's business.

Arthur Chuff Chuff

Railway worker in Rhymney.

The Singing Stallion

He thought he was good at singing and with women.

Jones Balloon

Given the name after the visit of a
V.I.P to the factory, when he said
"Now don't let me down boys."

Splinters

A rugby player who spent most
games on the bench.

DO YOU KNOW A
NICKNAME?

Tell Roy Noble about it - perhaps it may be
included in the next volume of Welsh Nicknames

Nickname

....

Reason for the nickname

....

....

....

Your name and address

....

....

....

Please send to Roy Noble, BBC Radio Wales,
Llandaff, Cardiff CF5 2YQ

Thank you for buying this Western Mail & Echo Ltd publication. We hope you have enjoyed it, and as a special offer we have included this voucher giving 10% discount off your next book purchase.

Order any book from your local retailer or Western Mail & Echo Ltd and receive 10% off the R.R.P.

This offer applies only to books published by Western Mail & Echo Ltd. However, you may purchase your books from either Western Mail & Echo Ltd or your local retailer.

Simply present this voucher when you purchase your next Western Mail & Echo Ltd book.

To the retailer: Complete the retailer coupon overleaf to claim your discount and send it back to the Book Department, Western Mail & Echo Ltd., Havelock St., Cardiff CF1 1XR. Wales, U.K.

RETAILER REDEMPTION COUPON

To the Retailer: Please accept this voucher as 10% discount off the R.R.P. of any Western Mail & Echo Ltd book. For a full refund of this 10% discount, please send this completed coupon to:

The Book Department, Western Mail & Echo Ltd., Thomson House, Havelock Street, Cardiff, CF1 1XR.

When redeeming vouchers please ensure that all the details are completed. Only fully completed coupons are valid. No photocopies.

RETAILER DETAILS

Name ....

Address ....

....

....

....

....

Town ....

Post Code ....

Tel No. (daytime) ....

Contact name ....

PURCHASER/CUSTOMER DETAILS

Name ....

Address ....

....

Town ....

Post Code ....

Tel No. (daytime) ....

Book title purchased ....

R.R.P. ....

Discount given ....

POSTAL ORDER FORM ONLY

Order your next books or audio tapes by post for a 10% discount. This applies only to additional purchases.

To: **THE BOOK DEPARTMENT, WESTERN MAIL & ECHO Ltd., HAVELOCK STREET, CARDIFF CF1 1XR. WALES**

Please rush me the following:

(Please print name and address CLEARLY)

Name...

Address..

Postcode ....

Tel: ....

Please debit my credit card

⊔⊔⊔⊔ ⊔⊔⊔⊔ ⊔⊔⊔⊔ ⊔⊔⊔⊔

(expiry date) ⊔⊔⊔/⊔⊔⊔

Name: Signature:

(CAPITALS)

Please allow 21 days for delivery on U.K. addresses or call into the Western Mail & Echo offices in Cardiff. Alternatively visit your local retailer. For further details ring 01222 583441.

Please note! Post and package applies to U.K. orders only – for overseas P&P add £5 per item.

BOOK TITLE	ISBN No	Qty	Price	Total
Gren's Guide To Rugby	09504042 68		£4.95	
Ponty an' Pop	1-900477-01-7		£4.95	
Images of Cardiff	18598302 85		£5.99	
In the Footsteps of King Arthur	09504042 41		£7.95	
A Guide to the Dyfi Valley Way	1-900477-00-9		£7.95	
TAPE TITLE			Price	
Great Moments in Wales			£4.95	
Great Games in Welsh Rugby			£5.95	
Total quantity/cost				
Special Discount Less 10%				
Add Postage & Packing @ £1 per book				
Total remittance enclosed				

CARTOON ORDER FORM

ACCOUNTS DEPARTMENT, Western Mail & Echo Ltd.,
Thomson House, Havelock Street, Cardiff CF1 1XR. Telephone: 01222 583441

Wing-nut
Williams

For personalised and signed copies of your favourite Gren cartoons, please complete this form, not forgetting who your cartoon is for!

Size A4 (approx. 21x29cm / 8x11ins), printed on 160gsm buff matt art paper. Copy unframed.

Your name & address

Name ....

Company Name ....

Address ....

....

Town ....

Post Code ....

Tel ....

Please debit my credit card

☐☐☐☐ ☐☐☐☐ ☐☐☐☐

☐☐☐☐ (expiry date) ☐☐/☐☐

Name: ....
(CAPITALS)

Signature: ....
(PLEASE SIGN & SEND TO ABOVE ADDRESS)

To . . . .

Best Wishes GREN

Page Nº	Cartoon reference BLOCK CAPITALS PLEASE	Quantity @£8.00 ea.	Amount £
17	WING-NUT WILLIAMS	1	£8.00

Postage & packing included to UK only. For overseas orders add £1.00. Alternatively orders can be collected from the Western Mail & Echo Ltd. at Thomson House.
(Please allow 28 days for delivery in the UK)

GRAND TOTAL *Please enclose your remittance and make cheques payable to Western Mail & Echo Ltd*